HERALDRY

HERALDRY

by Theodore
Rowland-Entwistle

Illustrated by Jim Dugdale
and Charlotte Styles

GRANADA PUBLISHING

Published by Granada 1984
Granada Publishing
8 Grafton Street, London W1X 3LA

British Library Cataloguing in Publication Data
Rowland-Entwistle, Theodore
   Heraldry. – (Granada guides)
   I. Title
   929.6   CR21

ISBN 0-246-12333-8

Printed in Great Britain by
Collins, Glasgow

Contents

What is Heraldry?

Heraldry came into being in the early 1100s when knights started wearing armour which completely covered them. A knight in full armour could not be recognized, so for identification people started to paint bright devices on their shields and on the cloth surcoats they wore over their armour to keep the sun off. It became the custom to pass these devices on from father to son, and they soon became family properties.

As more people began using such devices, it was necessary to keep records of them and to control their use in order to prevent duplication. The kings who ordered such records to be kept gave the job to their heralds, which is how the term 'heraldry' came into being. Because the devices were displayed on surcoats they came to be known as 'coats of arms', and from that comes another name for heraldry, armory. Today heraldry is most widely used in Europe and former European colonies.

These are the arms of Viscount Hereford, the premier viscount of England. His family, the Devereux, have held the title of viscount longer than any other family. Walter Devereux, who fought in France for Henry VIII, was created the first viscount in 1550. At an earlier time the family of Bohun had the title. The simple design of the shield shows that it is a very early coat of arms.

Arms of England

Arms of Scotland

Arms of Wales

Arms of Eire

Arms of Northern Ireland

Countries have coats of arms which are usually based on those of early rulers. The English coat of arms has been borne by England's rulers since Richard I, and Scotland's arms date back to Alexander II. The Welsh dragon and the harp of Ireland are also very ancient. The arms of Northern Ireland date from the creation of the province in the 1920s.

7

Heralds in History

Heralds were originally messengers. The ancient Greeks had such messengers, known as *kerykes*, and like later heralds they also had various ceremonial duties to perform. The Romans also had heralds, whom they called *fetiales*. One feature of these early heralds, and later ones, was that they were granted permanent safe conduct. They could go between enemy rulers to conduct negotiations (or deliver messages of defiance) secure in the knowledge that they would not be harmed.

Another duty of a herald was to proclaim his lord and master's rank and titles on ceremonial occasions.

The heralds of the early Middle Ages had similar duties to those of the Greek and Roman heralds. They took part in negotiations for royal marriages,

When a castle was being besieged, the attacking army used to send a herald to call on the defendants to surrender.

which were very important in those days because they often meant an alliance of countries as well as of the two people who were getting married. In deciding on who was a fitting bride for a prince, or indeed for any high-born nobleman, heralds had to be expert in *genealogies* – that is, family trees.

So when coats of arms came into general use the heralds were the obvious people to control them and make sure there were no duplications.

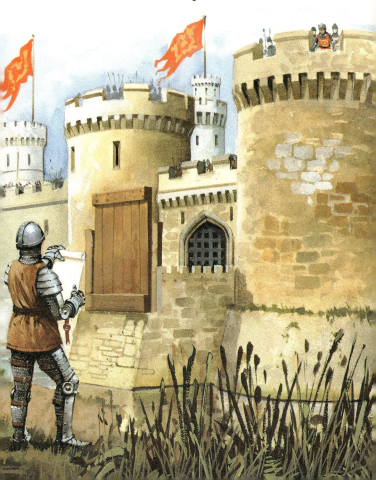

The College of Arms

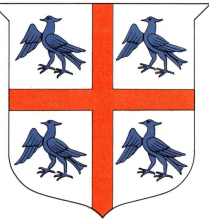

The College of Arms has its own coat of arms. The college building is in Queen Victoria Street in the City of London, and the red cross on a white ground reflects not only the City's arms but also the flag of England. The birds are doves.

Heraldry in England and Wales comes under the control of the College of Arms, which received its charter from Queen Mary I in 1555. The College alone has the right to grant and design coats of arms. It comes under the control of the Earl Marshal, who also – in name at least – presides over the High Court of Chivalry. This court rarely sits, but it can deal with legal questions concerning coats of arms.

The most senior officers of the College are known as Kings-of-Arms, of whom there are three: Garter, Clarenceux, and Norroy and Ulster. Next in order of seniority are six Heralds with the titles of Windsor, Chester, Lancaster, Somerset, York, and Richmond. Heralds have assistants known as *pursuivants*, from the French word meaning following. The four Pursuivants at the College are Rouge Croix, Rouge Dragon, Bluemantle and Portcullis. From time to time extra heralds are needed, and these are known as heralds or pursuivants extraordinary. Since the reign of William IV the annual salary bill for the heralds has been £252.16!

In addition to granting new arms, the heralds decide whether people are entitled to use arms already in existence. They also take part in, and often organize, state ceremonies such as coronations, royal funerals, jubilee celebrations and royal weddings. They have also taken part in ceremonies in Commonwealth countries and the United States of America.

Above: Garter King-of-Arms is the most senior of the Heralds.

Left: The post of Earl Marshal is hereditary, and has been held by the family of Howard almost continuously since 1483. It is now borne by the Dukes of Norfolk.

The Court of the Lord Lyon

The arms of the Lyon office are dominated by a lion, one of the Scottish emblems, holding a thistle in one paw. The upper part of the shield contains the Cross of St Andrew, who is the patron saint of Scotland.

Scottish heraldry comes under the control of the Court of the Lord Lyon, in Edinburgh. Although it is the equivalent of the College of Arms in London, it is organized very differently. It is headed by Lord Lyon King-of-Arms, who ranks as a Great Officer of State, and the post is not hereditary. The Court has complete control over the right to bear arms, and also over the succession to Chiefship of a clan. The Lord Lyon sits as a judge in the Court to decide questions relating to heraldry. It is a punishable offence under Scottish law to use somebody else's coat of arms.

The Lord Lyon has three Heralds and three Pursuivants under him. Until 1867 there were six of each, so there are 12 titles available, some of which are always in abeyance. The titles of the Heralds are Rothesay, Albany, Islay, Marchmont, Ross and Snowdoun, and those of the Pursuivants are Carrick, Unicorn, Dingwall, Kintyre, Bute and Ormond.

The names of successive Lords Lyon are known from 1452, but the post is much older. The Lyons were originally *seannachies* (genealogists) to the Scottish kings. At a coronation the Lyon's duty was to recite the new monarch's pedigree, thereby proclaiming his right to the throne, though this was often the cause of dispute and warfare.

The Lord Lyon wears a red robe on ceremonial occasions. Below (front), he is shown wearing a tabard bearing the royal arms of the Scottish sovereign. Behind him stand two Heralds and a Pursuivant, also wearing their tabards.

The Language of Heraldry

Heralds use a mixture of English and old French terms to *blazon* (describe) a coat of arms. It is very accurate, and once you understand the language it is possible to draw a coat of arms just from the written desciption. To begin with, heralds use the term *dexter* and *sinister* to describe the right and left sides of a shield – right and left being from the wearer's point of view, rather than from an observer's. The language is described more fully on pages 20–21.

The colours in which a shield is painted are called *tinctures*. They comprise two metals: *or* (gold) and *argent* (silver); five colours: *azure* (blue), *gules* (red), *sable* (black), *vert* (green), and *purpure* (purple); and nine furs, all-over patterns based on animal skins: *ermine, ermines, erminois, pean, vair, vair*

SHIELD SHAPES

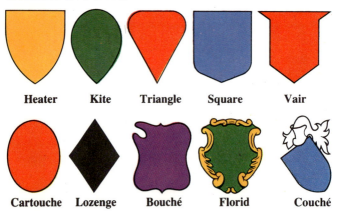

Heater   Kite   Triangle   Square   Vair

Cartouche   Lozenge   Bouché   Florid   Couché

METALS AND COLOURS

Heralds do not put one metal on another, or one colour on another. This rule was adopted to give maximum contrast and so make the design of a shield easy to identify.

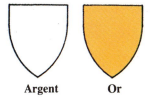

Argent   **Or**

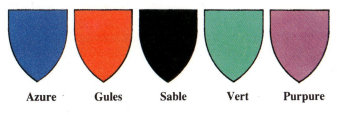

Azure   **Gules**   **Sable**   **Vert**   **Purpure**

FURS

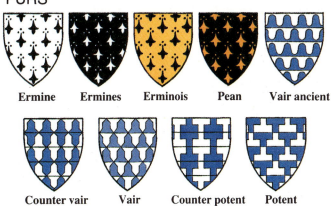

Ermine   **Ermines**   **Erminois**   **Pean**   **Vair ancient**

Counter vair   **Vair**   **Counter potent**   **Potent**

ancient, counter vair, potent, and *counter potent.* All these tinctures are shown on these two pages together with some of the basic shapes of shields commonly used. The most popular is the *heater,* shaped like the sole of an iron. The *lozenge* is used by women.

15

Ordinaries and Divisions

Designs on a shield are called *charges*. The simplest charges were made by painting the reinforcing metal bands on a shield in contrasting shades. These simple charges are known as *ordinaries*, and there are nine of them: *chief, fesse, bar, pale, bend, saltire, chevron, pile,* and *cross*. One or more of them can be found in most coats of arms. A number of other charges are derived from them, for example *paly* from the pale, *quarterly* from the cross, and *bendy* and *bendlets* from the bend.

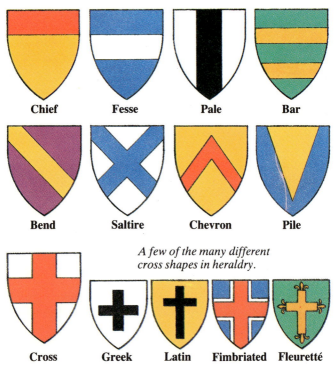

Chief   **Fesse**   **Pale**   **Bar**

Bend   **Saltire**   **Chevron**   **Pile**

A few of the many different cross shapes in heraldry.

Cross   **Greek**   **Latin**   **Fimbriated**   **Fleuretté**

OTHER CHARGES AND DIVISIONS

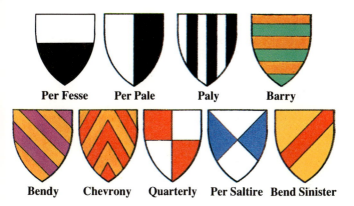

Per Fesse **Per Pale** **Paly** **Barry**

Bendy **Chevrony** **Quarterly** **Per Saltire** **Bend Sinister**

Lines dividing one part of a shield from another are called *partition lines*. A shield divided in half horizontally is *per fesse*; if vertically, *per pale*. There are number of different partition lines, and each one has a special name, as shown below.

PARTITION LINES

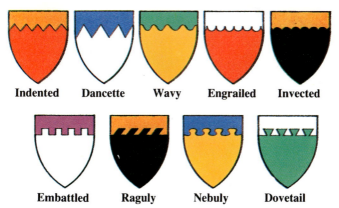

Indented **Dancette** **Wavy** **Engrailed** **Invected**

Embattled **Raguly** **Nebuly** **Dovetail**

Subordinaries

Subordinaries are a group of basic charges often used in heraldry. They are considered to be less important than the ordinaries, but they are just as frequently employed.

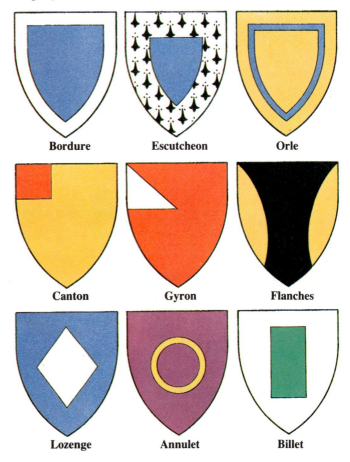

Bordure	Escutcheon	Orle
Canton	Gyron	Flanches
Lozenge	Annulet	Billet

Roundels

Roundels are a group of subordinaries whose names vary with their tinctures. The two based on the metals are shown as flat discs, while those based on colours are shaded to appear spherical. The *bezant* (or) was probably called after the Byzantine gold coin of that name, while the *plate* (argent) comes from the Spanish word *plata* meaning silver. The origin of the names for the roundels in colours is more obscure, but is based on old French: *torteau* (gules), *hurt* (azure), *pellet*, also called *gunstone* or *ogress* (sable), *pomme* (vert), and *golpe* (purpure). The *fountain* gets its name from the association of such wavy lines with water in heraldic blazons. The *annulet*, a ring, was sometimes called a false roundel – that is, one that has had its centre removed.

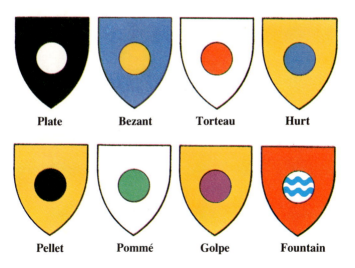

Plate   Bezant   Torteau   Hurt

Pellet   Pommé   Golpe   Fountain

Describing a Shield

When heralds blazon a shield, they give the tincture of the *field* (background) first, followed by the charges and their tinctures. The example on this page shows the way in which a simple charge is built up. You will notice that any charge is followed by the adjectives describing it, for example a *cross gules*, not a *gules cross*. This follows the rules of French grammar.

If there is more than one charge, the most important is given first. For example, a white shield

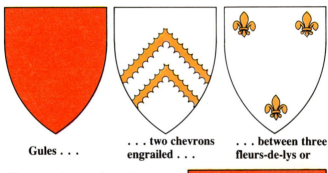

Gules . . .

. . . two chevrons engrailed . . .

. . . between three fleurs-de-lys or

The three pictures above show how the imaginary coat of arms on the right would be built up in a heraldic blazon. Gules describes the field; then come the most important charges, two chevrons which are engrailed – that is, they have fancy edges. Finally come the three fleurs-de-lys, while 'or' gives the tincture of all the charges.

20

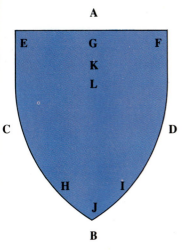

The various points of a shield are described as follows:

A   The Chief
B   The Base
C   The Dexter Side
D   The Sinister Side
E   The Dexter Chief
F   The Sinister Chief
G   The Middle Chief
H   The Dexter Base
I   The Sinister Base
J   The Middle Base
K   The Honour Point
L   The Fesse Point

Heralds use these points to indicate the positions of some charges.

bearing a black lion surrounded by four red stars would be described as: *Argent, a lion rampant sable between four mullets gules*. The word 'rampant' refers to the attitude of the lions: for this and other terms concerning lions see pages 30–31.

When a shield is divided up, each part is described separately. In practice this division usually means that the shield combines two or more coats of arms. To take a well-known example, the British royal arms combines the arms of England, Scotland and Ireland, the English arms being shown twice.

Heralds have specialized terms for describing the way in which charges are depicted. For example, *proper* means that the charge is painted in its natural colours. *Semé* means that the field is scattered with small charges, for example, *semé of roses*. An animal is said to be *armed* if its teeth, talons, horns or claws are shown, often in another colour: a *lion gules armed azure* is red with blue teeth and claws.

21

A Full Achievement of Arms

A coat of arms with its charges is the most important heraldic possession. But it is only part of a full *achievement of arms*, which contains up to 15 different heraldic devices. Most commoners, that is people without titles, have in addition to the shield a *helmet, mantling*, a *wreath*, a *crest*, and a *motto*. They may also have *supporters*, a *compartment*, a *cri-de-guerre*, a *standard*, a *badge*, and *augmentation*. The knight of an order of chivalry adds the *circle and badge* of his order, a more senior knight adds the *collar* of his order, and a peer adds a *coronet*. Many of these devices are shown in the achievement of the Duke of Norfolk, the Earl Marshal, opposite.

If you are entitled to a shield you are also entitled to a helmet; for a commoner it is of plain steel with the visor closed, while a peer has a silver helmet. The mantling hangs down the back of the helmet, to keep off rust and hot sun. It is usually shown cut and jagged, as it would be after a battle. The wreath is a twisted skein of silk on which the crest sits. In battle a crest on the helmet was another mark of identity. The motto is usually shown under the achievement.

EXAMPLES OF CRESTS

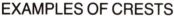

Crest of Bacon

Crest of the BBC (British Broadcasting Corporation)

Crest of Shakespeare

22

Coronet

Crests

Mantling

Wreath

Helmet

Arms

Supporter

Motto

Arms of the Duke of Norfolk

Supporters are figures placed either side of the shield, often animals, such as the lion and unicorn of the British royal arms. The compartment is some scrollwork or other design for the supporters to stand on; it often bears the motto. Augmentations are additions to an original coat of arms, granted by the sovereign in recognition of some special service. The cri-de-guerre (war cry), standard and badge are not displayed with the arms, but the emblems of knighthood are, an example being the collar of the Order of the Garter in the royal arms.

The Royal Arms

The British royal arms are probably the best known in the world. They have been unchanged since Queen Victoria came to the throne in 1837, but they had many variations before that. The first king whose arms are known was Richard I (1189). In 1340 Edward III quartered them with the lilies of France to stake his claim to the French throne. He used *France ancient* – multiple lilies; from 1405 the shield bore *France modern* – three lilies only. The Stuarts, from 1603, quartered these arms with those of Scotland and Ireland. George I added his family arms of Hanover in 1714, and in 1801 the French lilies were finally dropped.

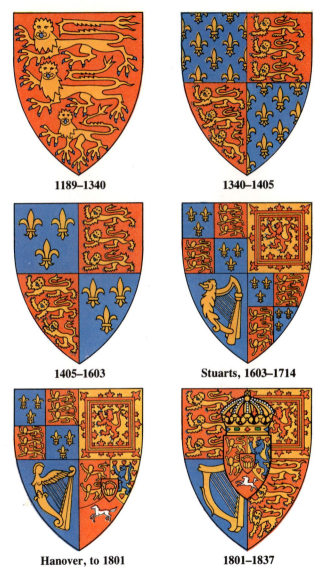

1189–1340

1340–1405

1405–1603

Stuarts, 1603–1714

Hanover, to 1801

1801–1837

25

Heraldry in Warfare

In medieval battles, heraldic devices distinguished the two sides.

Warfare in the Middle Ages was very different from modern warfare. For one thing, armies were very much smaller. Historians calculate that there were fewer than 20,000 men in action at the Battle of Hastings in 1066. As a result of this small size, commanders had a much closer relationship with their soldiers. In those days too kings, princes and great lords were the army commanders. They led their forces into battle, and their personal courage was essential to make their men fight harder.

Combat was at close range. Although archers could fire their arrows across distances up to 350 metres, most of the fighting was done with swords or spears, hand to hand. A battle of this kind was a very confused affair, a jostling affray of foot soldiers and cavalry all mixed up together. For this reason herald-

ry was all-important, because it enabled the warriors readily to distinguish friend and foe.

Knights wore their brightly painted surcoats and carried their shields. Their supporters often wore some kind of badge, or the colours of their leaders, to show which side they were on. The leaders' banners bore the same devices as their shields, and served as rallying points in the thick of the battle. These banners have survived to become the regimental colours of today. Although the colours are not carried into battle in the same way as they were, they are still treasured by the soldiers of these regiments. The idea of medieval badges still survives in the cap and shoulder badges worn by soldiers of many countries. They are also painted on tanks and other military vehicles.

Charges

Almost anything can be used as a charge in heraldry. Human beings are rare, though hands, such as the Red Hand of Ulster, are not uncommon. An unusual device is that of the Isle of Man, three human legs joined at the thigh, from which comes the old heraldic joke that 'the arms of Man are legs'.

Animals and birds are among the most common charges. Weapons of war and articles associated with riding and falconry are also used, as are the sun, moon and stars. The moon can be shown in three positions, called crescent, increscent and decrescent. There are also knots, some of which, such as the Stafford knot and Wake knot shown here, are associated with particular families. The commonest ship is a stylized galley called a *lymphad*. It was popular in Scottish heraldry.

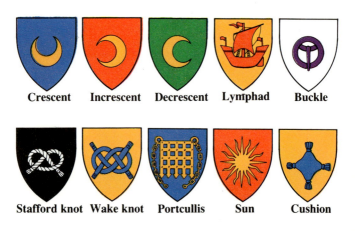

Crescent   **Increscent**   **Decrescent**   **Lymphad**   **Buckle**

Stafford knot   **Wake knot**   **Portcullis**   **Sun**   **Cushion**

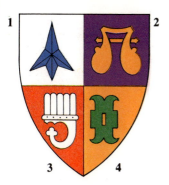

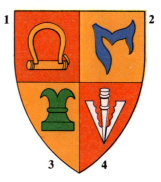

Left: The four devices shown here are (1) a caltrap, a four-pointed object used to lame horses; (2) a bouget, or waterskin; (3) a clarion, a wind instrument somewhat like a pan-pipe; and (4) a millrind, a bearing for a millstone.

Right: Shown here are (1) a fetterlock, a form of shackle and padlock used for securing prisoners; (2) a maunche, a lady's sleeve; (3) a chess rook or castle; and (4) a pheon, the head of a dart.

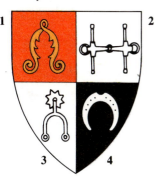

Left: These objects are connected with horses – (1) a barnacle, used to curb unruly steeds; (2) a bit – the type used varies; (3) a spur, the emblem of knighthood; and (4) a horseshoe.

Right: Guttés are drops, and their names vary according to their tincture. Guttés de larmes (1) are azure, representing tears; guttés d'eau (2 and 3) are argent, for water; (4) guttés de sang (gules) represent blood. Guttés d'or are drops of gold.

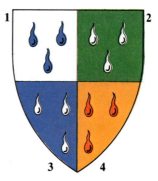

29

A Pride of Heraldic Lions

The lion rampant has been the royal emblem of Scotland for hundreds of years. Its first known use was on a seal of Alexander II in 1235, but it was obviously in use long before that date. The border round it is equally old.

The lion, the King of Beasts, is the animal most often blazoned in English heraldry. Lions are found in various attitudes, described as follows: *rampant*, erect with one paw on the ground; *passant*, walking to the dexter with one paw raised; *guardant* (any position) looking out of the shield; *reguardant*, looking over its shoulder; *statant*, with all four feet on the ground; *sejant*, sitting down; *couchant*, lying down; *dormant*, asleep; and *salient*, similar to rampant but with the paws differently placed. At one time any lion not rampant was described as a leopard, because it was thought to be acting like a leopard. The three lions borne by English kings used to be called leopards.

Reguardant

Passant guardant

Lion's head

Statant

Passant

Sejant

Couchant

Dormant

Salient

Above: This painting of Geoffrey of Anjou comes from an enamelled brass plate on his tomb, dating from 1151. It is the earliest picture of anyone with a shield of arms. Geoffrey was the son-in-law of Henry I of England, the father of Henry II, and the ancestor of all later English rulers. He was the first of the Plantagenets.

31

Other Heraldic Beasts

Bear's head

Boar's head

Eagle

Besides lions, valued for their strength and as a symbol of courage, other animals used as charges since the earliest days of heraldry include boars, deer, dogs, rams and bulls.

Birds have always been popular subjects, such as the eagle, the symbol of many German and Russian families. The sport of falconry led to the use of the falcon, while the swan and the peacock, stately birds valued as food, were also popular. A curious choice was the parrot, which has the heraldic name of *popinjay*.

As if there were not enough real animals – and today almost every animal has been used by some-

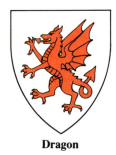
Dragon

Wyvern

Cockatrice

The gryphon is one of the emblems used by the City of London. Gryphons such as this one, with a shield bearing the City's arms, are positioned to mark the City boundary.

The gryphon was invented in the Middle East about 4000 years ago. It is basically an eagle, with ears and the body of a lion. It was a favourite object for decorating buildings and was known in ancient Greece. It was probably introduced to heraldry by crusaders returning from Palestine.

one – heralds invented fabulous monsters derived from classical mythology. The *gryphon* or griffin is shown above. The *dragon* is a scaly beast with bat-like wings and four legs. The *wyvern* is a species of dragon with only two legs. It sits on its tail. The *cockatrice* is like a wyvern, with the addition of the head, comb and wattles of a cock. The *opinicus* has a gryphon's head, a lion's body and a bear's tail. The *unicorn* has a single horn, a horse's head and body, and a lion's tail. The *enfield* has a wolf's body with a fox's head, and eagle's talons on its front legs.

Opinicus

Unicorn

Enfield

33

Heraldic Puns

Heralds have always been remarkably fond of puns when choosing suitable arms for people. They like to make the choice of a device appropriate for the person, and something that matches his name is an obvious choice. Arms of this kind are sometimes called *canting arms*, or *armes parlantes*. The arms of the Queen Mother's family, Bowes-Lyon, for example, include bows and lions. Sir Thomas Lucy, the squire who tried young William Shakespeare for poaching, had a coat of arms which showed three lucies (the old name for pike); and apples formed the device on the shield of Applegarth. The heralds were slightly more subtle when they chose a device for a medieval family named Hopwell: their shield has three rabbits on it!

Other examples of punning heraldry are the three boars' heads (swine) of Swinburne; roses for Rossel; shells for Shelley (the family of the poet Percy Bysshe Shelley); the ram, for Ramsey; and the lamb for Lambert. Often the pun depends on French or Latin. Arundel has three *hirondelles* (French for swallows); Fitz Urse, a bear (*Ursus* is Latin for a bear); De Heriz, a name later corrupted to Harris, a

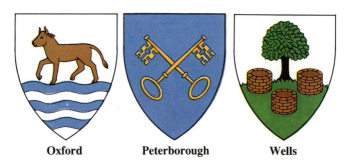

Oxford   Peterborough   Wells

34

Bowes-Lyon

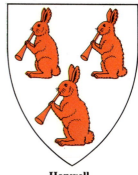

Hopwell

hedgehog (French: *hérisson*). Foreign heralds used puns too: the shield of Ferdinand of Castile and Leon, the Spanish ruler, bore castles and lions.

The same kinds of puns are found in the shields given to places. Oxford shows an ox crossing a ford; Wells has three wells; Peterborough shows the traditional keys of St Peter, keeper of the Gates of Heaven. In Old English the name of the town of Beverley meant 'beaver stream', and the shield shows both a beaver and a heraldic river.

Lucy

Applegarth

Tournaments

Heraldry really came into its own at tournaments, the sporting fights in which knights proved their courage and skill during the Middle Ages. Only the nobility were allowed to take part, and the heralds were kept busy checking the credentials of would-be combatants. A tournament was an occasion not only for the display of skill, but also for the display of heraldic devices and banners. Tournament armour was even heavier than battle armour, to protect the knights as far as possible. The combatants were supposed to use blunted lances and blunted swords but, even so, many men were seriously wounded or even killed.

Two knights in combat during a tournament in the Middle Ages.

The main feature of a tournament was single combat between mounted knights, each trying to unhorse the other with his lance as they charged. Sometimes there was a *mêlée*, or general combat, between two groups of knights. When they were unhorsed the knights fought on foot.

The ground where a tournament was held had various names. It was sometimes called a tilt-yard, from the old meaning of the word to tilt, that is, to ride and thrust with a spear. An alternative word for tilting was *jousting*. The tilting-ground was often called the *lists*, from an old word meaning a boundary, which referred to the fences around the ground.

Marriage and Descent

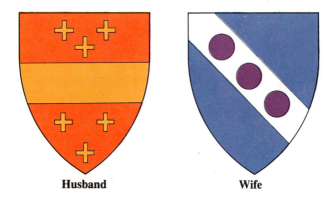

Husband   **Wife**

The more complicated coats of arms are the result of marriages, and heralds have various ways of showing these alliances. The easiest way to explain the rules is with the imaginary examples on these pages.

Up to the 1400s a husband showed his wife's arms by *dimidiation*: each shield was cut in half, and the two halves placed together, the husband's on the dexter side. This produced some extraordinary results, such as lions with fishes' tails. The more

Dimidiation

Impaling

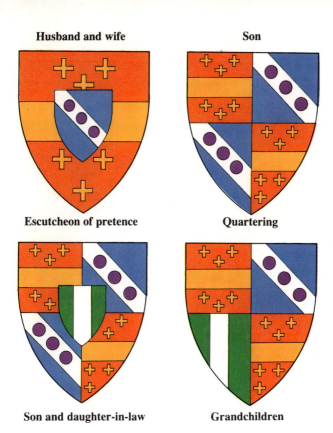

Husband and wife   **Son**

Escutcheon of pretence   **Quartering**

Son and daughter-in-law   **Grandchildren**

usual method is by *impaling*, in which the two coats are each squeezed into half the shield.

However, if the wife is an heiress (which in heraldic terms mean she has no brothers and succeeds to her father's estates), the husband carries her arms on .a small shield in the middle of his own, called an *escutcheon of pretence*. Their children can then add the mother's arms to their own by *quartering*. Two stages of this are shown. If the wife is not an heiress, the children revert to the father's coat of arms.

Hatchments

When somebody entitled to bear arms died, it used
to be the custom to display his arms over the main
door of his house. The arms were painted inside a
lozenge-shaped frame, which was known as a *hatchment* (a corruption of 'achievement'). Many old
hatchments still survive because it was usual after the
funeral to transfer the hatchment to the local church,
and there some still hang.

If you see such a hatchment, you can deduce quite
a lot about the person it commemorates. If the whole
of the background is black, then the person who died
was either unmarried, a widow, or a widower. If the
dead person was a husband or wife, the arms of the
couple would be impaled. If the husband died, the

40

A hatchment with an all-black background, showing that a single person, widow or widower has died. It was usual to carry the hatchment in the funeral procession to the local church, and after the funeral to display it in the church as a memorial. Many old hatchments still survive, especially in churches close to large stately homes.

Hatchment of single or widowed person

background behind his half of the shield was painted black, and the other half was white. If the wife died, the background behind her arms would be black, and that of the husband white. If you see a hatchment on which the wife's side is black in the upper half and white in the lower, then you will know that the husband has died, but he had two wives, the first being dead.

The frame of a hatchment was always painted black. The main part might be painted on canvas, or on a wooden panel.

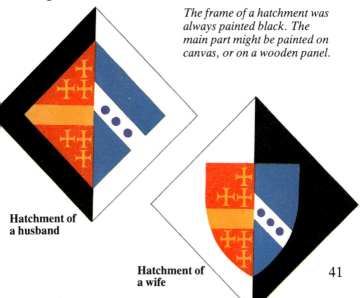

Hatchment of a husband

Hatchment of a wife

41

Difference and Distinction

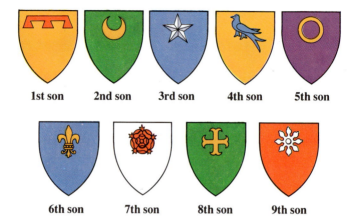

1st son **2nd son** **3rd son** **4th son** **5th son**

6th son **7th son** **8th son** **9th son**

When members of a family are entitled to bear the same arms heralds add marks to their shields, which are known as marks of *difference* or *distinction*. Marks of difference, also called marks of *cadency*, are used in particular by sons. The eldest son places a label of three points across the top of his father's shield, as shown in the illustration top left on this page. If he has a son while his father is alive, the

In Scotland the usual mark of cadency is a bordure, but sons must ask the Lord Lyon to matriculate (grant) such differenced arms afresh each time. Bordures are assigned in various tinctures. A bordure compony (alternate sections of a colour and a metal) is used as a sign of illegitimacy.

Plain bordure

grandson uses a label of five points. The second son uses a crescent, and there are marks for other sons up to nine, as shown above.

Members of the English royal family all use labels of three points, argent. The Prince of Wales has a plain label, but other princes and princesses have labels with symbols on them such as crosses or roses.

Marks of distinction are used where there is no direct descent by blood from the original bearer of the arms, or for illegitimate sons. The phrase 'bar sinister', often used to describe illegitimacy, is a nonsense since a bar cannot be sinister or dexter. It is derived from the French heraldic term *barre-sinistre*, which means a bend sinister. In the early days of English heraldry a bend sinister was often used to denote illegitimacy, it being a matter of pride to claim descent from a famous father – especially if he was a king. Generally the charge used was a *baton sinister*, that is, a bend *couped*, or cut short, at each end. Today it is usual to use a *bordure wavy*, but this has to be obtained by royal licence. An adopted child also has to obtain a royal licence to use the adoptive father's arms; the usual charge of distinction for adopted children is a pair of linked annulets.

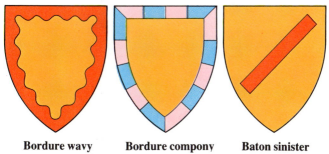

Bordure wavy   **Bordure compony**   **Baton sinister**

43

Corporate Arms

Heralds use the term 'corporate arms' to refer to arms granted to a *corporation* – that is, a body of people, as distinct from an individual. Cities, towns, counties, universities, colleges, city companies and other bodies all use arms, and have done since the 1400s. At a time when comparatively few people could read, arms – which could be readily identified – were of great value in labelling property, or as seals on documents.

Most of the towns of the British Isles have their own arms, and so did the historic counties until the reorganization of local government in the 1970s. Most of the present-day counties, and the regions that replaced them in Scotland, still use arms. A few, such as West Midlands and Strathclyde, use symbols more like trade marks.

Local authorities often display their coats of arms on the side of their public service vehicles.

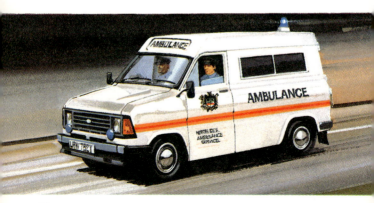

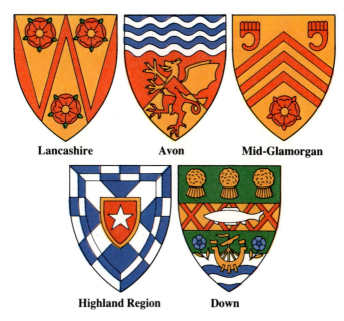

Lancashire   **Avon**   **Mid-Glamorgan**

Highland Region   **Down**

Many of the arms used by cities and counties are very old, and carry symbols which relate directly to the places and their history. London, the capital of England, uses the device of the English flag, St George's Cross, differenced with a sword in one corner. Liverpool shows the liver bird (pronounced

Bury St Edmunds

Liverpool

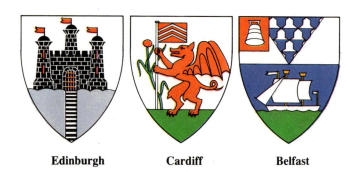

Edinburgh   **Cardiff**   **Belfast**

to rhyme with driver), the heraldic name for the cormorant. Edinburgh's arms show a castle, symbolizing one of the city's principal features.

Sometimes the arms of a place are associated with noble families. The arms of Lancashire show the Red Rose of Lancaster, borne by the royal family of that name during the Wars of the Roses. The three counties of North, South and West Yorkshire all display the rival White Rose of York.

The arms of Bury St Edmunds show a very interesting device: the 'attributed' arms of St Edmund, who was king of East Anglia, and was murdered by the Danes in 869. Edmund lived long before heraldry existed, but heralds gave (attributed) arms to all sorts of people who never had them, including Julius Caesar and King Arthur. There are even arms for Jesus Christ and Satan.

Universities all have arms, and so do the individual colleges of Oxford and Cambridge. A book, symbol of learning, is used as a device by many universities including the Open University, founded as recently as 1969.

Often the arms of the colleges of the older universities reflect those of their founders. Balliol College, Oxford, was founded by a Scottish princess, Dervor-

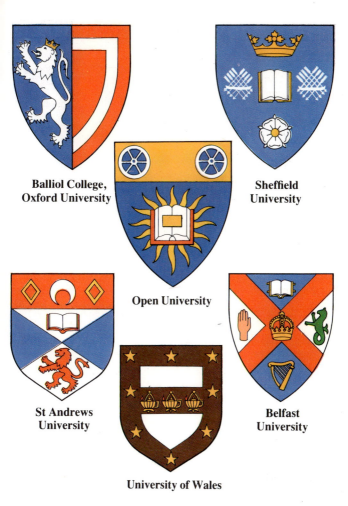

**Balliol College,
Oxford University**

**Sheffield
University**

Open University

**St Andrews
University**

**Belfast
University**

University of Wales

guilla, and her husband John de Balliol; their arms, impaled, are those of the college. Unusually, Dervorguilla's arms are on the dexter side, since she was the more important person. Their son, John Balliol, was king of Scotland from 1292 to 1296.

Churches and Companies

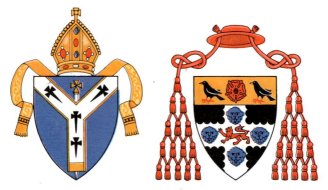

See of Canterbury **Cardinal Wolsey**

Abbeys, priories and dioceses of the Church have
had their own arms since early times. If a high-
ranking clergyman such as a bishop is entitled to bear
arms of his own family, he impales them with those
of the *see* (bishop's diocese or district) or other
Church body. The arms of Cardinal Wolsey, shown
above, display his own arms on the sinister side, with
those of his Church office on the dexter. The red hat
and tassels show that he was a cardinal. Wolsey's
own arms are also used by Christ Church College,
Oxford, which he founded in 1525. The arms of a
bishop or archbishop are surmounted by a *mitre*, the
pointed hat worn by a bishop on ceremonial occasions (see above left).

Companies and guilds have had arms for a long
time. The Drapers' Company of London, a City
guild, received their arms in 1439. Great trading
organizations such as the East India Company were
also given arms. In modern times the big public
corporations such as the BBC (British Broadcasting

BBC

Atomic Energy Authority

Corporation) and the United Kingdom Atomic Energy Authority have arms. The arms of the Atomic Energy Authority incorporate the heraldic device of a pile, a pun on the uranium piles used in nuclear power stations.

Other companies also apply for, and receive, grants of arms. Some of the major banks use them on their buildings and stationery. Barclays Bank used to carry on business at the sign of the Black Spread Eagle in Lombard Street, London, and now employ this as their device.

Barclays Bank displays this spread eagle device prominently on the walls of its many branches.

Inn Signs

The custom of hanging a sign outside a tavern or inn, usually a bush denoting a grape vine, dates from Roman times. Such signs were used in the Middle Ages and much later for other business premises too: for example, the 17th-century Fleet Street bookseller Daniel Pakeman carried on business 'at the sign of the Rainbow'.

The Red Lion was the badge of John of Gaunt, son of Edward III.

The sign of the Three Horseshoes was a symbol of the blacksmith's trade.

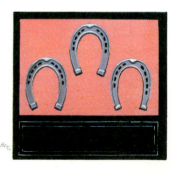

Many heraldic devices survive to this day as inn signs. An inn patronised regularly by a nobleman might well display his arms or his badge, or a loyal subject of a king might display the king's badge. For example, the Rising Sun on an inn sign was the symbol of Edward III and indicated the publican's support for his king. The Swan commemorates Henry VI, the Greyhound and the White Lion Edward IV, and the White Horse was the emblem of the Hanoverian kings. There are many King's Arms, and since the royal arms have varied over the years (see pages 24–25), it is often possible to tell in whose reign the pub was first opened. Some public houses display the complete arms of some local nobleman or landowner, such as the Abergavenny Arms at Tunbridge Wells in Kent. Others show the arms of various craft guilds, such as the Carpenter's Arms, found in many parts of the country. In the days before street numbering, public houses formed convenient landmarks in towns, and even today many bus stops are identified by inns.

The White Hart was the badge of Richard II, whose reign was marked by rebellion and unrest.

Some inn signs, such as the Robin Hood, indicate the existence of local legends.

Heraldry Around the World

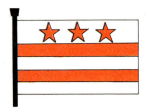

The flag of Washington, DC, (above) is derived directly from the family arms of George Washington (right).

Heraldry flourished all over Europe in the Middle Ages and is still practised in most European countries, even in some behind the Iron Curtain. It also spread to all the lands colonized by Europe, where it is still popular.

The people of the United States, most of whom had European ancestors, are interested in heraldry, even though the Constitution expressly forbids citizens from bearing titles – and heraldry often goes with titles. Yet the country has its own arms, and so do most of the states: Maryland, for instance, uses the arms of its original owner, Lord Baltimore, for its state seal and flag. Many American citizens have either established the right to European arms – of England, Scotland, Ireland or Spain – or have applied to the heralds of those countries for a grant of arms. Others have adopted arms to suit themselves. In 1967 an American College of Arms was established.

Although coats of arms originated with monarchies and nobility, many other republics besides the

The heraldry of Ireland formerly came under the control of Ulster King-of-Arms. His office is now combined with that of Norroy King-of-Arms, and deals only with the arms of Northern Ireland. In the 1940s the Republic of Ireland set up a Genealogical Office in Dublin Castle, with all the old records of Ulster King-of-Arms, and appointed a Chief Herald of Ireland. There are no other heralds or pursuivants in the Republic. The arms of the Genealogical Office of Ireland are shown on the right.

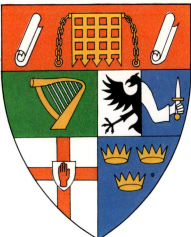

United States have organized systems of heraldry. South Africa, which used to come under British heraldic laws, became a republic and left the Commonwealth in 1961: two years later the country set up a state bureau of heraldry. The Communist republic of Yugoslavia has its state coat of arms embodied in its constitution, though in neighbouring Hungary the use of coats of arms has been banned.

Japan has its own system of heraldry, based on the 'mon', the badge of a noble family. It started in the 1100s, just as heraldry did in Europe. The devices were displayed on banners to identify soldiers in battle, and Japanese nobility used their personal mons on their garments and buildings, but not on shields. A typical Japanese mon is shown here.

Commonwealth Heraldry

In the days of the British Empire all the dominions and colonies had their own coats of arms. Many of these arms are still used today, even by countries which have since become republics.

Some commonwealth countries have had new arms since independence. These arms are granted by the College of Arms in London. The prime minister of each country negotiates directly with Garter King-

Canada

Australia

New Zealand

The arms of the three 'Old Dominions' are shown here. In the arms of Canada the arms of 'France modern' symbolize the French origin of parts of Canada. The Australian arms incorporate devices from the arms of the individual states, while those of New Zealand emphasize the importance of farming, mining, and trade to the country.

Newfoundland

Nova Scotia

Newfoundland, which used to be a separate dominion, had its arms granted in 1638. The supporters, not shown here, are Red Indians. Nova Scotia's arms are even older, being granted in 1625. The colony was at first closely associated with Scotland, as its name implies and the shield shows. New South Wales has a kangaroo as one of its supporters.

New South Wales

of-Arms and the heralds go to great trouble to devise arms suitable for them. For example, British settlers accidentally landed in Bermuda in 1609 when their ship, bound for Virginia, was wrecked there. The coat of arms of Bermuda shows a ship being dashed against the rocks.

Of the great dominions, Canada was the first to have independence and the first to have its own coat of arms. Each of the Canadian provinces also has a coat of arms. Australia, with its states and territories, also has arms, and so does New Zealand.

European Heraldry

Wars and revolutions have affected heraldry in Continental Europe much more than in the British Isles. In former times, as still in Britain, the monarchs of the various countries were the people who could award honours – coats of arms as well as titles. With the disappearance of most monarchies, the honours have gone too. A great deal of historic heraldry remains, however, and people entitled to bear coats of arms still take pride in them.

In France hereditary titles were finally abolished in 1852, when the Second Republic was established, but heraldry was allowed to remain. There is no controlling body, but the ownership of arms is recog-

Left: The arms of Norway's royal family have been unchanged since about 1300, when the axe was added to an earlier lion rampant. The lion is said to have been the device of Sverre, king from 1184–1202.

Right: The castles and shields in Portugal's state coat of arms recall events in the country's history. Portugal has only about a thousand coats of arms altogether. Two private bodies deal with heraldry.

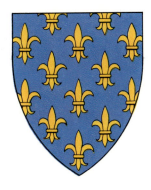

Left: The old royal French coat of arms, France ancient, dates from the 1100s and has fleurs-de-lys scattered all over. A new coat of arms with three fleurs-de-lys was adopted about 1365, and is known as France modern.

Right: Italy, as a republic, ignores heraldry, but the nobility have their own National Heraldic Council. The arms shown here are those of the Perriello-Zampelli family.

Left: The Spanish royal coat of arms has existed since 1230, when Ferdinand III united the two kingdoms of Castile (device: a castle) and Leon (device: a lion rampant), to form the present arms.

Right: Sweden's shield of three crowns is known as the Small Coat of Arms: the Great Coat of Arms quarters the crowns with lions rampant, and has an escutcheon bearing the arms of the current royal family.

57

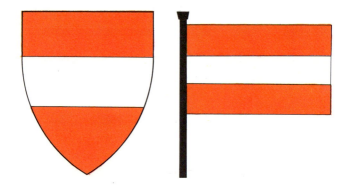

The archdukes of Austria, who ruled Austria for hundreds of years, had a simple, ancient shield: gules, a fesse argent. After Austria became a epublic in 1918 the new state retained their coat of arms to form the new national flag. The imperial eagle, dating from the 1100s, is also used.

nized by law: for example, a wine merchant who used somebody else's family arms on his wine bottles was sued and made to remove them.

In Belgium, which is still a monarchy, there are a great many nobles, and heraldry is controlled by a heraldic council. Sweden and Denmark also have state officials with heraldic powers, but most other countries do not. Portugal has a commission to deal with heraldry, and Spain has a chronicler of arms with the powers of a King-of-Arms.

Some idea of the complications that arise in European coats of arms can be seen in the arms of Charles of Habsburg. He became Duke of Burgundy in 1506 at the age of six, then King of Spain (as Charles I) in 1516, and finally Holy Roman Emperor (ruler of the German states) in 1519. His shield (opposite) combines the coat of arms of Spain with those of Austria, Burgundy, Brabant, Naples and other places.

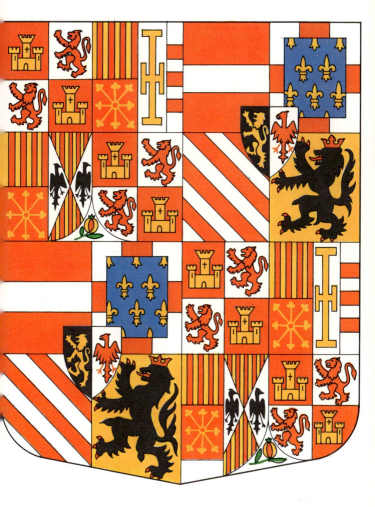

Coat of arms of the Holy Roman Emperor Charles V.

Glossary of Terms

Achievement Complete heraldic design.

Annulet Ring used as a CHARGE.

Argent Silver.

Armed Of an animal, having teeth and claws, etc.

Armes Parlantes CANTING ARMS.

Arms Heraldic compositions with their various CHARGES.

Augmentation An addition to an existing coat of arms to signify a special honour.

Azure Blue.

Bar Horizontal strip across a shield, covering about one fifth of its area.

Barry Divided into an even number of bars.

Base The lowest part of a shield.

Bearings The heraldic devices carried on shields.

Bend Diagonal strip across a shield, running from DEXTER CHIEF to SINISTER BASE. *Bend sinister* runs the other way.

Bendy Divided into an even number of bends.

Billet An oblong figure.

Blazon Another term for heraldic compositions.

Bordure A border around the edge of a shield.

Cadency Devices used to show the difference between members of the same family.

Canting Arms Those where a pun or play on names is used in selecting CHARGES.

Canton The first quarter of a shield.

Charge Any heraldic device.

Chevron Strip shaped like an inverted V.

Chief The upper third of a shield, sometimes slightly less.

Coat of Arms The complete heraldic composition on a shield.

Collar Part of the insignia of an order of knighthood, worn around the neck, and used in achievements of arms if the holder is entitled to it.

Colour The five colours used in heraldry are: AZURE, GULES, SABLE, VERT, and PURPURE.

Compony Row of small squares of alternate TINCTURES.

Couchant Lying down.

Couped Cut off cleanly.

Crest Device originally worn on a helmet, and now displayed above a coat of arms.

Dexter The right side of a shield, as seen from the point of view of the *holder*.

Difference An addition to a coat of arms to distinguish it from an identical one.

Dimidiated Cut in half vertically with one half removed.

Dormant Asleep.

Engrailed Having a wavy edge.

Erased Torn off with a ragged edge, the opposite of COUPED.

Escutcheon A heraldic shield.

Fesse Horizontal strip across the centre of a shield.

Field Background of a shield.

Flanches Curved sections either side of a shield.

Fleur-de-lys A stylized lily.

Furs Stylized patterns used as TINCTURES: ermine, ermines, erminois, pean, vair, vair ancient, counter vair, potent, counter potent.

Guardant Looking out from the shield.

Gules Red.

Guttées Drops.

Gyron Triangular division of the shield, like a wedge.

Impaled Joined per PALE.

Label Strip with pendants at the top of a shield to mark CADENCY.

Lozenge Diamond-shaped shield.

Martlet The heraldic martin, usually without feet.

Metal The two metals used in heraldry are OR and ARGENT.

Mullet A star.

Or Gold.

Ordinary A simple basic charge.

Orle Shield with its centre missing, charged on another.

Pale Vertical strip down the centre of a shield, about one-third of its area; *per pale*, divided in this way.

Passant Walking and looking forward.

Pile Wedge shape from the top of a shield.

Portcullis Defence for a castle door.

Purpure Purple.

Quartering Putting two or more coats in different quarters of a shield.

Rampant Erect, one hind paw on the ground, the others raised.

Reguardant Looking backwards.

Roundel Disc-like charge.

Sable Black.

Salient Bounding or leaping.

Saltire A diagonal cross.

Sejant Sitting.

Semé Scattered over the FIELD.

Sinister The left side of a shield, as seen from the point of view of the *holder*.

Supporter A figure, often an animal, that stands beside a shield as if supporting it.

Tabard Short garment, with sleeves, worn by heralds.

Tinctures The two METALS, five COLOURS and nine FURS used in heraldry.

Torse Twisted wreath under a crest.

Tressure A very narrow ORLE set round with FLEURS-DE-LYS.

Vert Green.

Note: Capitalized words denote a cross-reference within the glossary.

Index